GO FIGURE

GO FIGURE

Carol Moldaw

Four Way Books
Tribeca

for Miriam Sagan

Library of Congress Cataloging-in-Publication Data

Names: Moldaw, Carol, author.
Title: Go figure / Carol Moldaw.
Other titles: Go figure (Compilation)
Description: New York : Four Way Books, 2024.
Identifiers: LCCN 2024000679 (print) | LCCN 2024000680 (ebook) | ISBN
9781961897045 (trade paperback) | ISBN 9781961897052 (e-pub)
Subjects: LCGFT: Poetry.
Classification: LCC PS3563.O392 G6 2024 (print) | LCC PS3563.O392 (ebook)
| DDC 811/.54--dc23/eng/20240119
LC record available at https://lccn.loc.gov/2024000679
LC ebook record available at https://lccn.loc.gov/2024000680

This book is manufactured in the United States of America and printed on
acid-free paper.

Four Way Books is a not-for-profit literary press. We are grateful for the assistance
we receive from individual donors, public arts agencies, and private foundations
including the New York State Council on the Arts, a state agency.

We are a proud member of the Community of Literary Magazines and Presses.

CONTENTS

"Which I is *I?*"

— Theodore Roethke, "In a Dark Time"

Visiting the River After Having Moved Away

The treads of my boot soles
hard pack block print
ideograms in river mud.

Which will outlast which:
the melancholy of returning here
or the pattern made from it?

On Being Mused Upon

Reading his poems, you recognize yourself
in intermittent isolated images—your scent,
your nape, your hair, an arrangement of flowers
you once placed at the center of a long table.

It adds to evidence that you are being seen,
which is not, you hope, the same as being watched,
a thing you don't want. Still, you wonder
whether the piecemeal *you* and *she*
resemble at all your version of who you are.

You may be seen but your nature is to feel
disappearingly visible as vape smoke,
as the scentless rings your daughter perfects
as she begins to separate her identity from
you both, from how or how not she is seen.

Go Figure

In her and her and her I saw myself.
In carved sandstone, a voluptuary,
my neck coiled to face my back, my back
twisted to pinch and raise for inspection
a small patch of almost-out-of-reach skin.

One foot planted, the other on toe,
my toes on a narrow ledge high up
the temple's façade. I'm unfazed
by gaze of mason, acolyte, or tourist.

And in her, also slightly coiled, rising
out of the bath under a painter's gaze, I saw
myself stepping over the tub's rim, sideways
into the easel like a towel. You call me
by the painter's name: a Lautrec. A Degas.

Myself in veined marble, my towel now
draped like a veil. Or etched, in a notched
crosshatch illusion of fishnets. Hewn
in block, impaneled in canvas, versions
sketched, filmed, celluloid, digitized—.

Countless iterations find me poised
as if alone at the mirror examining eye,
lip, brow: brush and palette in hand.

The mirror goes back to grit, a sand
that can't reflect but absorbs the noon sun
I peer up into, as into a museum's directed
and calculated light, as into a church's
perpetual dusk, cinema's blackout velvet.

Painter and Model (I)
after Lucien Freud's *Painter and Model*

Because she paints barefoot, she's barefoot in his painting
of her painting. Well, not painting, but modeling for him
as the painter she is and gazing toward her ostensible model,

splayed nude on a battered brown leather Chesterfield.
Well, not gazing: her eyes, as he painted them, are downcast,
the lids closed. If they were open, it seems by the bowing

of her head that she'd be looking at the model's outthrust knee—
though what the viewer notices first and foremost is what
the paintbrush idling between her clasped hands is angled toward:

the model's resting uncut cock. Both her inner and his outer gaze
are ambiguous, distanced; his, attending somewhere beyond
the painting he's in—perhaps focused on the back of the canvas

being painted as he lies there, or on the fanatical painter
(not her, standing at his side, who he did, in fact, model for,
but the one outside the frame who positioned, checked,

repositioned them both, on and on, just so . . .) or beyond him
and, in a reverie of the imagined future, onto us, our scrutiny.
Akimbo, one knee rests on the couch's pockmarked back

while the other extends over its edge, the weight of his heel
on the floor, his curled toes pointing toward the same heap
of squeezed-out paint tubes and crisscrossing brushes

that her right foot is on the periphery of, her toes pressing
on a tube that's oozing olive green. To me, this—
a bottom left-center tangent made by the intersection

of lines each set of toes invisibly extends—is the painting's
not-so-secret heart. Her smock dress, used as her paint rag,
is its own action painting; the cornered walls, a fresco's undercoat.

Painter and Model (II)

Toggling between the backlit blank screen
and palm-filtered early morning light,
I keep rubbing the same flat stone of thought,
comparing myself to an artist I admire
who wrote of how, painting a self-portrait
of herself painting, she remembers sitting
for portraits of herself her lover painted,
his artful assertions of blunt dominance.

She's more single-minded than I, more ascetic—
solitude, self-denial, intrinsic to her calling—
but we both hate being pinned like a prize
specimen to someone else's corkboard,
tagged as his *muse* with the subcaption
artist [read for me *poet*] *in her own right* . . .
a slyly disguised diminishment
of who and what we know ourselves to be.

No one is ever asked to model for a poet.
No one's lips are scrubbed or limbs realigned,
so I've avoided that particular power struggle.
Poets prefer to cast our muses sidelong looks,
to downplay awareness of our scrutiny.
I'm drawn to interiors and still lifes

and intimate, window-mediated landscapes,
no figure indicated beyond dashes and dots.

Isn't every poem, though, every painting,
no matter what, in the end also a self-portrait?
One eye always looking inward and one out;
ears attuned to discordant frequencies vying
within range: the oscillating table fan;
the swooping pitch of isolated birdcall;
and, like the incoming tide or a thought
turning over, palm fronds sighing in the wind.

Struck Dumb

My muse: made mute
by all that words entail,
enigmas I assumed
answerable in detail.
How endlessly minute
each minute is, subsumed
when a relative absolute
and silence dovetail.

Agra, December 2008

Shrouded in mist
up to its trinity of domes

and attendant minarets,
the fabled double tomb

relaxed into the sky
as if marble and air

mixed together formed
an amorphous solid.

To tour the famed
mausoleum, we waited

in separated security
lines all morning

and just like at home
the women's line

was laboriously slow:
inured, we suffered

each purse's ransacking
as the men moved

ahead, accelerated
by slapdash pat-downs.

At the end of the line
would be a keyhole view.

From the ramparts,
soldiers shouldering

sniper rifles surveilled us,
shifting their sights

degree by degree
across our puny multitude.

Stirred up out of mud
by girls with sticks,

mosquitos made me wish
I wore a hijab, while glad

I wasn't semi-wrapped
in a midriff-exposing sari.

I understood no one
I eavesdropped on

until out of its chrysalis
the opalescent silhouette

of arches, domes, and spires
emerged like a magic trick,

and it *was* incredible
as it spoke coolly of love.

Mumtaz and Jahan

Some say both spouses died of poisoning.
Of their fourteen children, the last she bore
was born on a battlefield; at least seven died
in infancy or young; two of them killed
at least two others. Years after her death,
one son imprisoned his father, her widower,
who had built a mausoleum, the Taj Mahal,
in her honor, her tomb and cenotaph
centered under the dome. One daughter lived
with the imprisoned father until he died.
He had planned to build his own mausoleum
across the Yamuna but his son stopped him.
Instead, Jahan was buried next to Mumtaz,
to the side. Yet wasn't the Taj truly his
(no name of any architect survives),
his immortalizing art upstaging her?

Raccoons

On my way to water the strawberries
at dusk—I gardened in those days—
I saw a raccoon clasping the outdoor spigot
like a sailor's wheel, using both paws
that seemed more and more like hands,
as it kept twisting until water gushed
out of the copper nozzle and it drank.

I hadn't thought of it in years, not even
after I saw another raccoon, high-stepping
the coyote fence midday with a limp vole
overhanging its mouth. Such a singular sight,
I had to tell you, and blurted it out as soon
as I saw you, a piece of domestic gossip
like the first crocus or noisy neighbors:

common property, like so much in marriage—
a small business, a friend called it, down to
the cooked books. Only later, after I spotted
the raccoon sauntering through a line
in one of your poems . . . only after the pressure
cooker of my displeasure caused you to recast
your raccoon and vole as skunk and mole,

did I flash on the one I'd seen decades before:
its lack of furtiveness, the air it had
of being within its rights, the way it took its time
to retrace its steps to turn the water off.
—Or did it amble on and let the water run?
No copyright protects idle talk, you might have said,
or: *The imaginarium of marriage knows no bounds.*

Time Zones

for Arthur

From inside the cabin, we watched deer
cross the dry lake bed and ripple toward us.

At first, we thought the deer might be elk,
an idea we liked as we don't have elk at home,

but head-on and up close, a deer herd
is almost as mesmerizing as an elk gang.

It's hubris to test the limits of infinitude,
so even after twenty-three years—halfway

between china and silver, aster and iris (or iris
and yellow rose, depending on the source)—

we try not to test each other's patience.
Sometimes a tide of reserve still washes over me.

Later, after dusk, I went to sleep in your arms.
The next day, scrambling across the lakebed,

I found, in crevices of dried mud, three shells
that I wrapped in Kleenex to bring to my desk.

One's finely ridged, curled tight as a fern frond;
one's the pincer part of a crab claw,

no bigger than my thumb; one's stretched
so thin and wide at the open brim that it chips

when lifted. Too small to seal against my ear,
it transmits no wave, no word, no sound:

> *three speechless oceanic mementos*
> *aeonian time zones from the sea.*

Family Values

"Perennial first-nighters," reads one caption
of my parents on the society page—
one of many newsprint photos they saved,
this one taken when I was twelve.

With a fur jacket draped over her shoulders,
and sporting pale chiffon palazzo pants,
my mother swans in a 3/4 pose—my father
in his tux a little stouter but as faux-relaxed

as Cary Grant. They lived it up, but never,
as they put it, *beyond their means*—a point
they made sure to drive home. And never
the fastest in their crowd—no kick worth

the risk of wrecking the life they'd made.
Still, as they said good night, re-enumerating
the bedtime rules—my father, halfway
out the door, already doing a soft-shoe.

Lessons

Taught as a girl to inquire
after a man's day, to affirm
with nod or smile what he says
went right, to flutter the stray
hand off shoulder or thigh
and emit a full-scale range
of fluted laughter, to feign
disbelief, inspire confidence.
Taught not how to embellish,
but to be myself embellishment;
in attentiveness and inattention
assume the same rapt mask.

Argument

Anytime we were caught in a bind,
really, it's nothing, we were taught to say,
as if unperturbed. I had to learn

how to imply and infer, and only later
could I bring myself to state outright.
Even now, to admit *bad feelings* shames me

and I'd rather glide over or elide them,
tacitly denying meaning to feeling
as if what's unremarked can't wound.

My argument with myself is the same
as my argument with the world: the same
disappointment, misapprehension,

disgust, disbelief. To parse it out, as now,
means every day to practice inflecting
a once-forbidden tense, *the present imperfect*.

Plover

With high-pitched, steady beeps,
like a backhoe backing up,

the plover screeched its alarm,
warning us off as we drew near

to float our towels to the sand
and bayonet the umbrella's

point in deep. Jim came on
the nest when he put down

the basket. Four eggs, protected
by driftwood and a row of little rocks.

Facing the sea, we half watched
the paddle game he played

with Sarah. Where was Arthur?
Kindly leaving us to ourselves

to talk of *whatever*: the cost
of life, of art, what to let go,

what keep. Olivia, you boast,
channels everything—rage,

fear, grief—into wall-scale
drawings precise as etchings:

no need (for now) for shrinks.
The plover had calmed down,

the buffer our excess stuff
created around her earning us,

if not trust, then a muted truce
and suspension of disbelief.

Behind us, sand dunes, bluffs;
before us, a late midsummer sun,

the kelp-flocked, shimmering sea:
a moment unguarded, prelapsarian—

or so it seems when I look back,
no longer heedless of the plover's chiding.

Northern California

Bulbous ropes of kelp the tide stranded.
Sandstone sea-break cliffs; eucalyptus groves.
A hammock strung between redwoods.

Up-scuffing dust with the pointy tips
of my riding boots, walking down to the barn
at camp, the Montecito Sequoia Camp for Girls.

Lifting the canvas flap and leaning out
of the top bunk in my flannel nightgown
to whiff cold air and be dazed by stars.

Shiny saw-toothed leaves of the live oaks
scattered through hills tawny with foxtails.
Camellia bushes; oleander; bougainvillea.

A bluff of salt-pocked Monterey cypresses
twisted in the same configuration, like '50s teens,
the boys, with windblown ducktail flattops.

No sooner had I finally let on to myself
that this was my psyche's landscape
than it burst into hellish, unquenchable flames.

Night Piece

Disoriented after we moved, I'd stumble
on the equally insomniac moon

all hours of the night, rolling
from window to window, inching north

as it traveled west, and slowly deflating
as if pinpricked by the burr of a star.

No matter what shape it was in,
directly overhead the moon eluded me

until a skylight would narrowly capture
its brilliance heading for the drive.

From our new entry's glass panels
I'd watch my old pellucid friend glide

across the canyon and gild the Jemez
before it sank like a coin in a slot,

leaving me to find my way by feel
to my side of our newly unfamiliar bed.

Reverberance

Rubbed with beeswax paste
to a high, soothing shine—
these walls, sharply planed,
slightly curved. The surface
of the plaster, as if lit
from within and windswept,
like a gypsum dune.

Inside *windswept* is *wept*.
Reaching down, the weeping
willow's branches swept
the gravel of our tears—
willows at the old house
and those particular tears
past their known impact.

Here, the apricot bears fruit.
Bear scat gums the long grass.
Where horses used to graze,
deer doze and, when they flee
our dogs, bump their hooves
on the hollow iron gate
that rings like an idiophone

and reverberates—through
the dogs' barking, through
the house and the sounds
we make living in it, the clatter
and chatter, the electronics—
slaying noise, piercing silence,
a cymbal's clean strike.

Shoe Box

Busy little monkey mind at work
while I watch the dance of willow leaves
outside our window and remember
other bedrooms, the way I "recall"
past lives' vague but plausible camouflage.
One year, beneath a crackle-printed comforter
I fret about the future; another day,
fanned out on a terry-cloth chaise, I pine
for the past, for the bristle-haired troll dolls
I kept in a shoe box when I was ten
and the lined index cards on which I wrote
unconnected nouns over and over,
each a skeleton key keyed only to itself,
unselfconscious as a series of selfies.

Scales

I'm off in sixteen different directions
like a rhumb line, like the morphometrics
in a butterfly's decorative eye.

∞

Something's not right, I write,
which helps *me*, if not it.

∞

Symptoms are our goad and guide.

∞

This morning, last night:
aggravation, desire:
two different orders of *dirty looks*.

∞

Others may have experience of God:
interpretations, imaginings are what I know—

a crescent moon's hammock
slung low between two palms.

∞

To be absorbed in a trance
even of avoidance, I play solitaire—
game of wordless patience—

∞

Then let the house go dark;
light only the room I'm in.

Not a Clue

I've years of clues, and no clue
about the seductive voice in your head
telling you what, what not, to do.

Whether or not it's true,
you said that voice was shed.
I've years of clues, and no clue—

motherhood daunting as voodoo:
I'd need the skills of a Jedi
to know what, what not, to do—

or a saint—someone who knew
how *not* to try to pry you out of bed.
I've years of clues, and no clue.

Things revert to normal, as if on cue.
I know I've been misguided,
telling you what, what not, to do,

and zoned-out on the bedspread
feel the nausea of it anew:
I've years of clues, and no clue,
what, what not, to do.

Mindfulness Training in La Jolla

That summer of Pokémon GO,
from our sublet condo
to the seaside promenade,
the phone of every third person
held out like a Geiger counter,
a prospector's dowsing stick—
the phone like a dog on a leash
yanking its owner for a sniff.
One out of three, me at times,
zombie-walking the sunset,
letting the day and its unsolved
clinical complications dissolve,
no second-guessing progress,
except through the Pokédex.

One session, asked to stand
with eyes closed the length
of time we think a minute takes,
the circle of parents and teens
is half game, half compliant. Lost
in non-thought, I'm last to sit.
Another day, our group gets split:
one division forms a gauntlet
the others single-file through,

and those pressing in pelt those afoot
with scalding reproaches
as bad as the worst bombardment
anyone hears in their head,
so we all know what it's like.

Evenings I streamed *True Blood*
and tried not to brood too much
or ask questions too hard for us.
At night, car lights lasered through
the crack in the velvet curtains
while the streetlights winked
and shimmied as patrons cast out
from the Tiki Lounge tetherballed
the lampposts, the noise careening
right at us before fading away.
One night, a woman, by herself
in the street, howled, raged, keened
and sang. A bug on its back,
I writhed in the loosened sheets.

You Have the Tools, Use Them

Meanwhile, a deer staggered
halfway up our drive
and collapsed on the lawn,
most likely struck by a car.
Robin left it on voicemail,
offering to remove the deer
in exchange for the meat
which she would butcher
then and there. The meat
was pristine, she said, so far
untouched by flies. She was
impatient to reach me, to get started
before a mountain lion found it.
At first, I heard only "deer"
and called back thinking
she just wanted to let me know
she was there with the dogs
and had seen some deer
rubbing against aspen bark,
chewing on orchard grass.
That was almost that, until—
this time making sure I really heard—
she went through it all again:
the corpse, the meat, the need to act.

Every Moment

The languor, the drive, the traffic, the parking,
the walking blocks to public beach access,
down past an atilt row of porta-potties,
dirt scruff shifting to sand under our feet;
the settling our stuff away from the water
to face the volleyballers, the being unable
to coax our puppy to nose at the tide,
the lounging until we get up and shake out
the sand, pack up, retrace our steps to the car;
the cars-at-a-crawl all the two-lane back,
the making a left across traffic to park, locking
the trunk—my purse, the keys, in it; miserable
at what I've done, at everything, wanting
a fight, wanting, but unable, to curb myself.

From the Roof Deck

From our temporary housing's rooftop deck,
I watch seagulls court on the roof next door,
the male cawing, hopping, wings exhaust flaps.
I'd never mistake *him* for a whooping crane,

but being amused is (almost) its own comfort.
From up here, I get how sharks can mistake
surfers bobbing upright on their streamlined boards
for seals, black wetsuits glistening like pelts,

but to catch a glimpse of Fourth of July fireworks
I have to drape myself around the chiminea
and list over the deck's edge. The display starts
with the sun, sizzling and sparking as it sinks.

No holiday required for *those* pyrotechnics.
Or for my burst of waterworks, now air-dried.

Olmec

The bone-crushing pain
of turning into a jaguar:
palpable in the shaman's
cleft head carved in basalt

or jade; in his down-turned
squared-off open mouth;
lips stretched and dilated
in birthing, in a scream.

Try to imagine yourself
crossing from one world
of pain into another, the quiet
needed to summon the fury

needed to catapult you over.
For the umpteenth time,
until entranced, I trace
a talismanic cascade of curlicues

copied from an old book.
Images smuggled out
from the border, TV loops,
stream into my closed eyes.

In no other world but this,
we watch as mother is again
and again torn from child,
no glyph known for repair.

Arthritis

"Save your hands," my mother says,
seeing me untwist a jar's tight cap—

just the way she used to tell me
not to let boys *fool around*, or feel

my breasts: "keep them fresh
for marriage," as if they were

actual fruit. I scoffed
to think they could bruise, scuff,

soften, rot, wither. I look down now
at my knuckly thumbs, my index finger

permanently askew in the same classic
crook as hers, called a swan's neck,

as if snapped, it's that pronounced.
Even as I type, wondering how long

I'll be able to—each joint in my left hand
needing to be hoisted, prodded, into place,

one knuckle like a clock's dial clicking
as it's turned to open, bend or unbend.

I balk at the idea that we can overuse
ourselves, must parcel out and pace

our energies so as not to run out of any
necessary component while still alive—

the definition of *necessary* necessarily
suffering change over time.

The only certainty is uncertainty, I thought
I knew, so ignored whatever she said

about boys and sex: her version of
a story never mine. It made me laugh,

the way she made up traditions, that *we*
didn't kiss boys until a certain age, *we*

didn't fool around. What *we*? What part of me
was she? No part I could put my finger on.

How odd, then, one day, to find her
half-napping in her room, talking first

to herself and then to me, about a boy
she used to know, her friend's brother,

who she kissed, she said, just because
he wanted her to. "Now why would I do that,"

she mused, distraught anew and so freshly
stung by the self-betrayal, I reached across

the gulf my father left, to her side
of their bed and stroked my future hand.

Stuttgart, 1971

The whole point of the trip was to pick up and drive
the chocolate-brown special edition Mercedes convertible
our father had ordered for our mother. From the factory
in Stuttgart they wanted to tour Loire Valley Châteaux.
While they schmoozed over schnapps with the head of sales
(*how could they?*), my sister and I—slumped, lumpen, our legs
slung over the arms of black leather cube chairs—waited for hours.
I passed the time imagining running away, even knowing
I'd always stop myself, afraid of turning the wrong corner
like we did in Amsterdam and finding myself slouched
with the women we saw in neon-framed windows.
Melancholic and melodramatic, I could hear sirens and then
a high-pitched scream that also woke my sister up
from whatever trance-life she'd found herself mixed up in.
How long our mother had been yelling and pounding
and which of us first recognized that the scream was hers,
I don't know, but finally we got up and followed the sound
until we faced our frightened, frantic, and angry mother
on the inside of a bathroom door she couldn't get unstuck.

On the Cusp

Don't forget me, she pleads, just as she's
quavering on the cusp of forgetting <u>me</u>.
She utters my birth time—our shared moment
of severing, my astrological starting point—
like a secret code, a charm, the combination
needed to open her built-in wall safe.
The gears grind. When she gets the time wrong
I correct her though I know I shouldn't.
She wants her daily horoscope read aloud:
Cancer, our mutual birth sign. What she says
she did wrong doesn't match what I think
but I let all that go, she did nothing wrong.
Look how we turned out. Aren't we your proof?
Don't forget me, she repeats. *Nine-oh-nine.*

Nature Hates a Void

The way water would flow into the hole made by displaced sand
when my mother and I sat on our knees at the beach, digging it out
and packing it into a pail together, just so, does aggression, like
water, come to occupy more and more of what's been excavated.

> Up from the wet sand or washing in
> with the incoming tide, water fills
> the newly scooped out hollow.

Thirdhand, my sister and I begin to hear about remarks we need
to apologize for. We seek out the individuals insulted and explain
that whatever it was, it wasn't meant personally, adamant that if our
mother knew she had said or implied such a thing to such an old,
dear, and valued friend, she would be mortified.

> She never perspired—let alone sweat—
> even as she strove to bestow to silver
> and to all her settings a silvery polish.

If we had in fact sat together digging in the sand, and if I had a
photo of the sandcastles we didn't build—turreted, flag-bearing,
encircled by moats that flooded with each incoming tide, just as the

adjacent sand pits did—my understanding would be the same: that the room for aggression increases with time and is filled.

> She played at the margins. Walking
> together at sunset, I never saw her let
> the tide slosh above her freckled ankle.

Even as stages of the disease are tinged with personality, soon what's left is tainted, *corroded*, made by extremity of expression disproportionate and perverse; and the self, the ordering principle, is displaced, or evaporates, made extinct, extinguished ahead of the body.

> Rust marks on iron filings
> where the nest was tucked in
> before it blew away.

My Mother Tells Me How It Works

I've seen this one before, just not through to the end.
Are you getting my messages? Here's where,
quartering an apple by the kitchen window,
he figures out the truth, pockets the knife
and runs. —Who pressed pause? Put it back on!

I never thought it would come to this, a neighbor-
hood of billionaires I can't comprehend.
Something's Got to Give Because I Said So.
You have no idea the things they do to me.

S__ bought off the board and so they honored her—
mistress of manipulation! That's how it works—
he never could admit that's how it works.
Is she still there when he comes back for her? . . .
I thought I could schedule sadness, boss it around.

The Busker

The puppeteer darted in and had his black cloth strung waist high,
pole to pole across the Métro car, before the doors even closed.
We were standing to the front of the carriage but a bit behind him
and could see only his right side, where a tattered, tricorn-hatted Punch,
his toes bobbing like a boxer's on the curtain wire, walloped
what must have been Judy dangling off to the left. We could see
the puppeteer's right foot thumping the pedal attached to a hi-hat,
the battered boom box that provided the rest of the soundtrack,
and the open cardboard box where the marionettes not in use
were collapsed in a heap as if they'd been shot and dumped in an
    unmarked grave.
After performing for three stops, he was gone as quickly as he'd come,
swooping up players, instruments, and set at the first squeal of the brakes
and out the automatic sliding doors the moment they fully opened,
his sateen cape fluttering stiffly like a flamenco fan in the rush of
    forced air.

Stuttgart Revisited

For years, Sue and I would collapse into hysterics
if one of us said "Stuttgart." We didn't have to say
"Mercedes factory" or "bathroom" or "Mom."
Just "Stuttgart" was enough to set us off,
remembering how once, left to fend for ourselves
in the showroom lobby, we ignored for a while
an insistent noise we eventually tracked down
a hallway to our soft-spoken, ladylike mother
screaming for someone to find and rescue her
from the dimly lit, narrow WC
she was trapped in, the doorknob off its spindle.
It was a shared stand-up routine we knew by heart,
but it's turned now that she's locked in again,
with no escape from her malady's creeping rust.

Particles

The wind's picking up just now,
she said—and then (I think),
It proves the sky is blue.

If, as I wasn't sure,
I'd responded *What?*, then
that alone would have addled her.

She has no construct of time.
I don't think she could say
the days of the week in order.

It's true that one day follows another,
but what gives them sequence?

And what, if not wind, stirs up
the sky's particles of color,
customizing day's mixes of blue?

Radical Acceptance

Yes, I say back, affirming that I too
cherish our recent heart-to-heart, although
I suspect the reference is to a talk
we never had. It doesn't matter to me
that our hallowed conversation is supposed.
It's meaningful enough to stand in for
other talks we didn't have or botched.
I'm not a word person, she often said,
usually in response to my questioning
whether some phrase I thought misused
expressed quite what she intended to say.
That we were at odds over issues of speech
aggravated—aggrieved, I think—us both
until the trucelike terms her brain imposed.

FaceTime

It makes a kind of cockeyed sense
that my mother lingers so robustly
long after her mind has left the party.
She was an überhostess after all,
and the caterers—no, the *caregivers*—
haven't gone home. She's forgotten
they need to get paid. (It's prearranged.)
A good thing Dad left money.

I came late to being a good daughter.
As a moral value, it didn't move me:
it involved too feudal a fealty.
What I wanted was safe passage,
diplomatic freedom to come and go
after the truce and treaty signing.
I sought dual citizenship, two passports,
primary residence in my own city-state.

Yet here I am, unsummoned, calling
nearly daily these last years, checking in
on FaceTime, so that even if we barely talk
we see each other up close from afar,
though mostly, and more and more,
my mother doesn't look at me at all—

her eyes shut or on her own image
in the corner of her screen, trembling.

Game Face

I've seen the thumbnail photo of the tantric massage therapist
in the back of the free weekly for decades.

With shoulder-length dirty blond hair and a red paste bindi
she looks alluring without suggesting youth or age.

I wonder if the photo has ever been updated and, if so,
whether she uses Botox. I wonder about her parameters;

a young woman's face, beautiful or not, is most often a blank slate,
the record of her experience written in a secret diary, in invisible ink.

To see the ravages of aging on one's face used to be inevitable.
Now it means one's taken a stance.

My resistance to tampering with my face is strong—
I'm not fair game for the hunting—

but would I have used Botox if I'd been in public relations?
Politics? Sales? If I myself had been "on the market"?

After menopause it was tempting to use migraines as an excuse
to try Botox—the same needle position for headaches and crow's feet—

but the migraines disappeared. Orgasm also dispels migraines.
I cultivate conditions conducive to orgasm:

I try not to take my partner for granted;
I buy the creams, the oils, the mood enhancers, the toys.

When, on a whim, I type *tantra* into the search bar
and click, sleek ergonomic couches appear

in seven colors of leather and the option of a brass stud trim
while, in voice-over, a woman gushes that tantra is *life-changing*.

The video features a couple demonstrating positions,
the couch their perfectly contoured tool and prop.

I might have been that limber once. (Like *redolent*,
I find *gushes* almost too redolent of female sexuality to use.)

For all their prowess, the couple on the website
look clinical, unarousing and, by their faces, unaroused.

Still, I think about where to put the magic couch
for our own demonstration of comically unbridled passion.

I don't want the same game face as a girl
but my face does seem to have lived more fully than me—

much in the same way that writing in fluorescent ink
is laid bare when put under UV light.

Meditation on the Veranda

Bliss—right now:
beneath a blue jade
vine's beaded bangs,

my sonar function
asleep, the *I* unstressed,
a syllable glided over.

(Except wherever
in the line it's placed,
the *I* is stressed.)

Behind me, a lipstick palm.
In front of me, the early
stages of sunrise,

the world before
highlighter's applied.

Makeup

for Sarah

I layer packing tape on the corners
and over the label of the box

of makeup palettes I'm sending you
as though the surplus correlates

to protective layers of love.
My first apartment that wasn't a sublet

or shared with another couple
was on Mass Ave., across from Martha.

Our friend Gus lived with Martha.
He moved in when he broke his leg

and didn't move out until long after
it healed. We're all still friends

but not as a group. The first
violent arguments I ever heard

came through a shared wall
early each Sunday, a hangover

from Saturday night. We didn't know
whether to call the police.

The first piece of furniture I bought
for myself was a massive metal desk,

army green from the Army-Navy store.
It barely fit in the rickety elevator.

We left it when we moved.
I think I owned one stick of kohl.

Mira showed me how to use it.
I thought her glass coffee cups

from Bowl & Board made her
more grown-up than I'd ever be.

Once a week, on Sundays, my parents
and I talked on the phone—always

the same, filled with their activities.
I wrote a poem about it for class,

filled with their activities, the way this,
written for you in your first apartment,

is filled with my memories, not yours.
Yours, I'll leave to you to make of them

what you will: in your own medium,
colored by your own daring and design.

873 Beacon

In my narrow tub, I thought I heard
you sigh the way you do when you come in
as I'm taking a long hot bath at home,
a non-sequitur sigh, contented, spent.
But *why* spent, *why* contented, you want me
to wonder, want me to ask, and I oblige,
sometimes lifting myself out of the water
before it's cooled, to dry off as we talk.
Why this lonely exile, the air exhales
on its own, to ask me in a huff of steam.
Be sure to kiss the cat and dog for me;
in my mind, I'm kissing you myself, but you
will have to find a way to make it stick
beyond a poem's needs and distances.

Audubon Circle

Three fixed points triangulate my Circle:
this room, its desk, bed, table, and couch;
two and a half, three, blocks west, a café
where daily I fill my thermos; the other side
of the trolley tracks, a neighborhood market,
runt of a national conglomerate's litter.
One crooked tangent leads off to the gym;
another, up Park Drive to the Fine Arts.

Before I knew the Circle's name, I knew it
as where Derek lived, though the only place
I went was his apartment, where I helped
type "Cul de Sac Valley" and, not yet more
than a silhouette of myself, sat as if at ease
on the blue couch, and tried not to stare
at the island watercolors framed in the hall
or the storyboards tacked to an easel.

Strangely, until Jeffrey pointed them out,
I didn't notice the lines from "The Season
of Phantasmal Peace" carved into the granite
planter curving around my block's corner:
". . . all the nations of birds . . ." perfect
for Audubon Circle, though I doubt if that

was on Derek's mind when he wrote
his lyric vision of the birds' seasonless flight.

Most days, winds circumnavigate the Circle
like a boy in a cape making a buzz saw sound
as he tilts his arms and runs amok to fly.
I say I'm doing research here, but research
into what? It's not until the day before I leave
that glancing skyward as I exit the café
I notice a sheet-metal swallow aslant a lamppost
as if lifting off its ledge or about to alight.

Eight birds in all, once I start looking,
each in a classic pose: the lilting swallow
I first saw, then a swan with folded wings,
a watchful crow, a hawk sniffing the wind,
a cardinal with its knee joint tucked.
The hummingbird about to dive beak-first
is as big as any, so it's hard to judge the scale,
and I can't tell if that's a whooping crane

or a stork courting above the spot
where the Green Line vanishes underground
on its way downtown and chug-chugs up

for the rest of its westward commute.
The wings are lifted but not fully outstretched;
the neck's mid-bebop and one leg's mid-strut.
The last bird's puffy-chested, caught at a run.
I think it's a partridge, quail or grouse—

I don't know. I've flown home by now.
Of all the phone photos I took
that bird's the blurriest. Who knows
when I'll be back. Just days ago, but before
the virus lockdown, the deaths incising
the pandemic's rising curve, I stood
transfixed and free on the street, looking up
dumbstruck, at a cast of cutout birds.

Dinner Guests

When wanting to walk, I circle the apple trees
behind our house until suddenly done

digging at gopher holes the dogs flop down,
crumbs of earth clinging to their paws like cake.

I might accelerate or change direction
as I round a lap at the dilapidated barn.

My repetitions have worn a path in the grass
and now I follow the path I unconsciously made.

I remind myself to look up at the mountain.
The blossoms took me by surprise at first

although the buds didn't flower all at once
but arrived like dinner guests, in lulls and bursts,

each bearing sweetly similar beribboned gifts
the way guests used to, and now flocks of them

are already drifting off in flurried gusts
the way we tended to, when we were guests.

Road Trip to Planned Parenthood

It rained overnight, refreshing the earth.
The air wasn't yet warm, the leaves

not fully unfurled. It was the height
of the virus, the first wave. With clinics

in seven states closed and ours booked,
we found one within a day's round trip.

I hadn't driven in weeks, for days
hadn't been past the bottom of our drive,

to pick up the paper at six and the mail at one.
We got a doctor's note in case the state's

border was sealed: "unable to schedule
time-sensitive procedure in-state, please

allow through." No one stopped us and we
made good time. Only one hazmat-suited

protester outside the two-block buffer zone
shouldered a sign stapled to a plywood cross

that proclaimed a woman's regret inevitable.
I kept both hands tight on the wheel

so as not to flip him off as we drove by.
In the parking lot, the cars were spaced

for social distance; the appointment
mostly by phone, each car a semi-private

glass-sealed intake room. At intervals,
the door opened to let someone in or out.

Up and down the path, everyone wore a mask
but with no legal necessity, not yet, to hide.

Richter Scale

If this were a *crowd-sourced blueprint for the resistance*,
it would tell you what action to take, but it won't,
it can't, isn't, I'm afraid, built that way. It wants,
instead, to daydream, to remember a sunset
when a bevy of deer vogued in the meadow,
all looking up at the same time while grazing,
all five tilting their heads at the same angle,
their tails held up like rattles about to twitch.

I scroll news the way my father followed stocks,
sensitive to the smallest tremor.
A seismograph, a lie-detector needle, my pen,
its doodles on the scratch pad. In slow motion,
who can tell which way things will fall? History,
in real time. The deer scatter when I blink.

Apologia

Were they really black leather cube chairs,
my sister asks, a pool lounge propping up
my corpse pose, a near-sleep
settling my breath, allowing me
to pretend not to hear. I'm uninterested

in whether they drank schnapps.
My standard for what's acceptable
is based on that famous passage
—is it in a letter, posed as a question?—
where Bishop wants to double-check,

to verify (or correct) her notion
about which way a goat's eye slits run,
across or up and down:
one of many types of things
I trust poems to get right.

Scavengers

One by one, six or seven ravens settle on the polished rim
of our front courtyard's bowl-cut stone fountain.

They cool their claws in the overflow, pecking
at the placid water, a hint of gurgle at its center.

From the window I see them convening, conversing,
but can't see why a flock is called an unkindness.

To get at that, I'd have to be out among the carrion.
When they leave, they lift off in one great rustle-snap.

First Days at the Conservancy

I'm looking out the window—Paula's window—
at the palms whose names I still don't and might never know,
trying to decipher
within the rustling, the susurrous rustling,
the distinct sound
the specific tonality
the wind stirs up in any one variety—
each palm its own instrument and the wind expert in them all—
but my ear can't pick out individual strands
from the overarching swell of the whole.

Poetry in the morning, planting in the afternoon:
I can almost imagine it
though it's not my way—
all around me the inner lushness of it manifest
in the palm garden's forested jungle,
wild with native palms and palms brought in,
underscored by Paula's understory
of ti plants and fern and myrtle spurge;
manifest in the sheaves of poems grown from syllable-seeds
and a custom mix of attention and inattention,
amassed into books and dispersed through the world.

Each palm William—or Merwin to me, who didn't know him—
each palm he planted he said was planting a poem
and surely he approved of the way the two words chime,
the inner pith of each with its own texture:
the palm's creaminess; the long *o* of a chanted *om*
in the first skipping stone of *poem*'s two-syllable drop
down its wishing well.
A palm, methodically transported
from pot to ground in the palm of the hand;
a poem growing as if with a flick of the fingers.

Keisaku **Palm**

for Miriam

Gravity brought down the palm frond's wide
and weighted sheath-end first: the bark,
still loosely attached like coarse black fringe,
lashed my ear when the stalk fell straight
from on high and thwacked the top of my crown.

On my way to the internet-connected garage,
taking the river-rock steps two at a time
to outrun the mosquitos, my laptop
compressed like a held-in prayer to my chest,
I was stunned into place and all the thoughts

that had squash-balled the box of my brain
since receiving your news, dropped like the flies
the shoemaker swatted—all in one blow.
It was like being clapped with the stick
a Zen master uses to wake a drowsy pupil.

I knew you'd know the name of the stick
and like the anecdote . . . comic relief
to round out my concerned, earnest reply.
Keisaku stick, you wrote back with a link:
a flat wooden slat, for focus or courage—

not necessarily a rebuke. To request it,
bow the head and place the palms together,
expose each shoulder in turn to be struck.
The crack when the pinnate frond detached
was loud and startling as close-by thunder.

What master was it who summoned the stave
down to school my cloud-crowded head?
On the lichen-splattered steps, the slap set off
a nerve wave of remembrance, a transmission,
your image from youth, "promiscuous with stars."

Meditation in the Open-Air Garage

Leaves have no choice
but to articulate the wind:

aspens like zills, aglint and atilt;
the willow, a lone zither.

Riffling the cottonwoods at dusk,
winds find me cushioned against

the concrete in the open-air garage,
facing the trees, the drive, the road,

the mountains up the canyon's
other side, until an onrush bellows

a mindless heartless ecstasy
through the empty sack of me.

ACKNOWLEDGMENTS

I gratefully acknowledge the editors and staff of the following publications and anthologies in which these poems first appeared, sometimes in slightly different form: Academy of American Poets Poem-a-Day; *The Account*; *The American Poetry Review*; *Connotation Press: An Online Artifact*; *FIELD*; *The Georgia Review*; *Green Mountains Review*; *Harvard Review*; *The Hollins Critic*; *Literary Imagination*; *The Los Angeles Review*; *The Massachusetts Review*; *NELLE*; *New Ohio Review*; *The New York Review of Books*; *On the Seawall*; *Plume*; *Poetry*; *Puerto del Sol*; *Subtropics*; *Virginia Quarterly Review*; *Vox Populi*; *The Yale Review*; *Zócalo Public Square*.

I would also like to thank the editors of these publications and anthologies, that reprinted poems, in some cases in translation: *Acanto*; The Columbia Granger's World of Poetry Online; *In the American Grain*; *New Humanist*; *Odes to Our Undoing: Writers Reflecting on Crisis*; *Plume Poetry 10*; *The Power of the Feminine II*; *Poetry Studio: Prompts for Poets*; *Sign & Breath: Voice & The Literary Tradition*; Women's Voice for Change: Poetry Sunday.

With gratitude also to Sonnet Coggins and Sara Tekula and everyone at the Merwin Conservancy, for an extraordinary month as a 2022 Artist-in-Residence.

With heartfelt thanks to the friends and colleagues who have read any one and sometimes many of these poems in draft and offered their invaluable insights: Jenny George, Jeffrey Gustavson,

Jeffrey Harrison, Elizabeth Jacobson, Ilya Kaminsky, Dana Levin, Tyler Mills, Jim Moore, and Jenny Oliensis. And, as always, to Arthur Sze.

And with great gratitude to Cecily Brown for allowing me to use "Untitled (After Bosch and Boldini)" as the cover of *Go Figure*.

And, finally, with deep appreciation to Martha Rhodes, Ryan Murphy, Hannah Matheson, and everyone at Four Way Books.

Carol Moldaw is the author of six previous books of poetry: *Beauty Refracted* (Four Way Books, 2018); *So Late, So Soon: New and Selected Poems* (Etruscan Press, 2010); *The Lightning Field*, 2002 winner of the FIELD Poetry Prize (Oberlin College Press, 2003); *Through the Window* (La Alameda Press, 2001), also translated into Turkish and published in a bilingual edition in Istanbul (Iyi Seyler, 1998); *Chalkmarks on Stone* (La Alameda Press, 1998); and *Taken from the River* (Alef Books, 1993). She is also the author of a novella, *The Widening* (Etruscan Press, 2008). She has received a Merwin Conservancy Artist Residency, a National Endowment for the Arts Creative Writing Fellowship, a Lannan Foundation Residency Fellowship, and a Pushcart Prize. Her poems, essays, and reviews have appeared widely in such journals as *The American Poetry Review, The Georgia Review, The New York Review of Books, The New Yorker, Poetry,* and *The Yale Review,* as well as many anthologies, including *Western Wind: An Introduction to Poetry* and *Contemporary Literary Criticism.* Along with Turkish, her poems have been translated into Chinese, Italian, Portuguese, and Spanish. A volume of her selected poems, translated into Chinese, is forthcoming from Guangxi Normal University Press in Beijing in 2025. She lives in Santa Fe, New Mexico.

We are also grateful to those individuals who participated in our Build a Book Program. They are:

Anonymous (14), Robert Abrams, Debra Allbery, Nancy Allen, Michael Ansara, Kathy Aponick, Jean Ball, Sally Ball, Jill Bialosky, Sophie Cabot Black, Laurel Blossom, Tommye Blount, Karen and David Blumenthal, Jonathan Blunk, Lee Briccetti, Jane Martha Brox, Mary Lou Buschi, Anthony Cappo, Carla and Steven Carlson, Robin Rosen Chang, Liza Charlesworth, Peter Coyote, Elinor Cramer, Kwame Dawes, Michael Anna de Armas, Brian Komei Dempster, Renko and Stuart Dempster, Matthew DeNichilo, Rosalynde Vas Dias, Patrick Donnelly, Charles R. Douthat, Lynn Emanuel, Blas Falconer, Laura Fjeld, Carolyn Forché, Helen Fremont and Donna Thagard, Debra Gitterman, Dorothy Tapper Goldman, Alison Granucci, Elizabeth T. Gray Jr., Naomi Guttman and Jonathan Meade, Jeffrey Harrison, KT Herr, Carlie Hoffman, Melissa Hotchkiss, Thomas and Autumn Howard, Catherine Hoyser, Elizabeth Jackson, Linda Susan Jackson, Jessica Jacobs, Deborah Jonas-Walsh, Jennifer Just, Voki Kalfayan, Maeve Kinkead, Victoria Korth, David Lee and Jamila Trindle, Rodney Terich Leonard, Howard Levy, Owen Lewis and Susan Ennis, Eve Linn, Matthew Lippman, Ralph and Mary Ann Lowen, Maja Lukic, Neal Lulofs, Anthony Lyons, Ricardo Alberto Maldonado, Trish Marshall, Donna Masini, Deborah McAlister, Carol Moldaw, Michael and Nancy Murphy, Kimberly Nunes, Matthew Olzmann and Vivee Francis, Veronica Patterson, Patrick Phillips, Robert Pinsky, Megan Pinto, Kevin Prufer, Anna Duke Reach, Paula Rhodes, Yoana Setzer, James Shalek, Soraya Shalforoosh, Peggy Shinner, Joan Silber, Jane Simon, Debra Spark, Donna Spruijt-Metz, Arlene Stang, Page Hill Starzinger, Catherine Stearns, Yerra Sugarman, Arthur Sze, Laurence Tancredi, Marjorie and Lew Tesser, Peter Turchi, Connie Voisine, Susan Walton, Martha Webster and Robert Fuentes, Calvin Wei, Allison Benis White, Lauren Yaffe, and Rolf Yngve.